Words are All I Have

Words are All I Have

Alexandra Sisam

RESOURCE *Publications* · Eugene, Oregon

WORDS ARE ALL I HAVE

Resource Publications
An Imprint of Wipf and Stock Publishers
199 W. 8th Ave., Suite 3
Eugene, OR 97401

www.wipfandstock.com

PAPERBACK ISBN: 978-1-5326-9299-4
HARDCOVER ISBN: 978-1-5326-9300-7
EBOOK ISBN: 978-1-5326-9301-4

JULY 16, 2019

To all of those that brought the words out through the love and the hurt and the fear and the whole myriad of emotions—thank you

And most of all to my people—donna, chris, steph and jeff—who stood by me through it all—there are no words enough for you. I love you

These are the words of
The heartache
The heartbreak
The only way for me
To make sense of my well of emotions
When they don't make sense at all
Please tread lightly

Love Alexandra

Contents

I am scared of what they will think

Will they think I am broken?

Will they think I am weird?

Will they think I copied her?

Will they run away from me?

Will I become a ghost?

Will he pretend as if he never knew me—like others have before

Will they even care?

Part 1

It Feels Like the End

I know I am the scum of the Earth
I know I am wrong in everyway
But why do you have to remind me
Constantly
Push me deeper into the dark pit where I live
Fighting and clawing to stay afloat

I would do anything for you
I would let you cut me in half if you needed
But you never see that
Only my fundamentally flawed self
That needs to be pushed deeper down into nothing

It hurts me

The way you come home everyday

Hurting

It hurts me

When you take that pain and turn it into fury

On me

And I take it

But deep down each time you snap

Each time you ignore

'Each time you yell

I feel like I should crawl back into the dirt where I belong

I feel like my existence is nothing

Like everything I do is wrong

And I hate myself

I hate myself for not stopping your hurt

I feel so alone

I am angry with you

My sister, my best friend

For taking your pain

Out on me when all I do is love you

I am so angry that you make me feel so worthless

And you don't even notice

You don't notice what your pain and your hurt is doing to me

You say you are so aware

Of how your actions

And your words impact others

But do you even see the way they cut me

The weight

It wants to push me down

And I want to go

I want to sink into the ground

No

Sink below the ground

To let gravity envelope my body

Crush me

Because even the ground isn't deep enough

Deep enough to stop the feeling

Stop the feeling of my soul being crushed

And my body pulling away

It is the dark place today

The place where everything seems heavy

And nothing makes sense

There is a shadow covering all that happens

Turning it from a normal event

Into something disheartening

Where the water feels it will swallow me whole

And I search for a hand

A hand to grasp onto and pull me out

To hold me close

And tell me the despair that I feel is not all that there is

But I can't ask for that

Can't ask for the help that I need

Can't ask for someone to join me in this feeling

So I sink alone and kick every once in a while

To keep myself afloat

I walk

A thousand steps

A thousand more

Because I can't sit still

And feel the pain crushing into me

Burying me alive in my own body

The pain that you will leave

One day

You will have to go

And I will too

And no amount of love between us

Can stop that

It is a tornado
Swirling around in my mind
And my body
With a pull attached to it
A magnetic force pulling me deeper into myself
Farther from the reality that makes sense
And closer to the despair and delusion
That coats everything in black
Turning each part of the world into something unable to bear
And sucking me in, deeper and deeper
So that it feels like I am drowning on dry land
And nothing can untether me from this place
Nothing can break the magnetic pull that holds me here
Because in the dark place
Logic does not exist

One moment. One day.

It's all it takes

To change everything

Everything I feel about myself

One feeling

One sensation

That is all

That word

      Sensation

          Situation

              Feeling

It takes me from too fat

To too thin and back again

It takes me from feeling prepared

To feeling like everything is wrong

It brings out emotion

That I need to keep hidden

The exhaustion pulls at me

And I want to fight it

Push myself back towards wakefulness

Where there is the illusion of control

Push myself away from the darkness, the fear, the nightmares

That plague me in sleep

The discomfort of being with myself

That only comes from lying down at night

When all of the preoccupations of the day

That stops me from feeling my body and my emotions

Slip away

Tossing and turning

I can't sleep

Waking as if in a daze

A feverish haze

With no fever and no illness

Just my body

Screaming at me

Trying to tell me something

That I cannot understand

So it doesn't stop

And the pain overtakes me

I can't sleep

I can't understand my own body

I sit in silence

In a room of people

Stoic. Smiling. Fine.

They cannot feel the hand twisting inside of me

Twisting and knotting and throbbing and aching

Like a stranger, an unknown outsider

Breaking into my sacred space; my body

Wreaking havoc

It feels like a force

So strong and overpowering

Seeking me out to bind my insides in twine

I want to scream and beg for help

As my body is assaulted from the inside out

And I can't

Because the assault is from within

A breach of contract between me and the body that keeps me safe

So I sit like a statue

My insides wrapped in barbed wire

Being twisted around a rusty knife

Accepting my body's revolt against the years of pain I have put it through

By hating myself and my body

I hurt today
Same as most days
Physical, emotional, spiritual
A constant rotation
Of pain in all forms
And as I sit here
Silently
Pain slipping through my body
I want to run
As far from my earthly home as I can
So I sip
My black tea
Made with herbs of the earth
And pray
That this will help keep me here
In this moment
In this pain
And keep my mind-
That wants to pull me away -
At bay

Invisible
I must be invisible
As I stand here
And you are with her
And she is with him
We all stand in a circle
Talking
But no one is talking to me

Once I was with him
And we talked and we laughed
And I felt loved

But I faded away
Disappeared from his vision
As I tried desperately to stay
In the corner of his eye
So he would choose me

Today is my birthday
They say it should make me feel good
Make me feel special

I don't feel special

Instead I feel ashamed
Ashamed of who I am
Ashamed I am not enough to make everyone happy
Ashamed that I disappoint people
Ashamed that my very presence can disappoint people
I am wracked with guilt about how undeserving I am of a day for me
How undeserving I am of the niceness of others

On other days I can fly under the radar
Hide from the deepest and darkest places inside of me

On my birthday—
As people bring attention to me
I am forced to bring attention to myself—
I can't hide from the truth of what I think about me

The hatred

The disappointment

The shame

It bubbles up with one simple action

Tearing up inside of me

Yelling

"Why?"

"Why do you do these things?"

"What is wrong with you?"

"How can you let this happen?"

"You are disgusting"

"Worthless"

"Disgraceful"

"You are nothing"

And as the yelling inside me continues

I feel a part of me

Trying to detach from my body

Fragments of my being, breaking off

Trying to escape the feel of being in my body

Breaking off so that they don't have to feel those same voices inside, yelling and causing so much shame

Breaking off so that they don't have to feel that same body trying to distract the voices by causing so much physical pain

The same body that tries with all its power to keep me safe

The same body that in my mind causes the hatred

The disappointment

The shame

How can this be my fault
It doesn't make sense
But a part of me
Screams that it is
If only I hadn't eaten that
If only I hadn't acted that way
If only I didn't do everything wrong
At every moment of everyday
If only I didn't do wrong
Maybe I would feel better
I would stop destroying myself
That is what it yells at me
Every moment of everyday
About every decision I make
And while it doesn't make sense
I believe it
It feels so real
Making me believe that I am wrong

How do I talk when all I can feel is the knives in my heart

And wrench in my gut

And the ache in my back

And the despair everywhere

How do I smile

Amidst the war inside of me

How do I love you

When I feel I can barely

Keep myself from breaking down

How do I go on

When my body feels so beyond my understanding—beyond my control

How do I do it?

How do I be here?

How do I be human when it hurts so damn much?

Maybe today is the day
The day I don't hear back
The day our conversations get less and less
The day you don't respond
The day you tire of me

I am waiting for it
Just waiting for that moment
Because how could you ever stay for me, care for me
I don't compare to her
I don't compare to anyone

And it hurts
Knowing this is coming
Willing you to still care about me
But knowing you will stop
They all stop

Why does this world have to break our hearts?
No matter what
We can't avoid it
And it breaks my heart
Just even knowing
That this will happen one day
That all who I love will leave to be somewhere else
And nothing I can do will stop it
I can't stop the millions of hearts
That shatter
Unexpectedly
Everyday
From this same sensation
The sensation of losing the love
And I crumble inside for each and every one of them
For each and every one of us

I can't look
I can't look at my own body
Down at my thighs
That feel they are busting out of their skin
Down at my stomach
That should never be allowed food
In the mirror
At my face, my hair
The bloating everywhere
The disgust, the hideousness
I can't look at my body—
My body that is

> *My home*

> *My protector*

Without disgust, judgement, hate
And more than that
I can't look at myself without shame
For feeling this way
About my own body

If I sit here

The voices will kill me

They will tear apart my body with my shame

With words like daggers

That would cut off layers of me if they could

Anything to make my body smaller

They make me want to take a knife and shave off layers 'til I am skin and bone and nothing else

In these moments—that feels like the only way

Anything to stop the voices, stop the shame, stop the pain

So I walk

Tears streaming down my face

And let the voices ravage my mind, my body, my soul

Walk and listen and cry

And hold on

Knowing that skin and bones will never quiet the voices

I know

I have tried

And now I walk

Can you see that I feel worthless?

That I feel broken

That I feel lonely

Can you see that I don't know what to do?

Or how to be

After so long trying to put myself back together

I don't know how to let you in, anyone in

I don't know how to be whole enough to be around someone else

Can you see that I am scared to be near you?

For fear that you start to see it to

There are so many things inside me
So many things that I don't understand
They lie just below the surface
But all I know is that I need to get away from them
That they can't come to the surface
I need to get away
Run away
In any way possible
From what is happening inside my body
From the emotions, the hurt, the physical pain
The despair, the hopelessness, the struggle,
The self-loathing

Part 2

The Inbetween

I write these words
Because I can't keep thinking them
Over and over
Because I can't keep feeling it
This empty space beside me
Looming, engulfing me
That no one can ever fill
Because I don't know how to let them

Over the years
I wanted to let them
Wanted to let anyone take away that emptiness
The emptiness, so full of darkness
And they came
And they left without another word
And the space
Felt emptier, darker, like it could never be filled

Now here I am
Alone
Wooed once by words
And left behind by none
Unsure of what to feel and who to feel it with
Because suddenly no one is right
Words hang empty in the air
They come
And the confusion sets in
And I run
Only letting them nudge that empty space
Never getting close enough to touch me
Before I disappear

I feel it all
Every ache, every pain, every sensation
In my body
Yelling and screaming
Something at me that I can't understand
I feel the trees around me
Their ageless wisdom and presence
Holding me up day to day
I feel the world, the flowers, the Earth
Beneath my feet
And I feel your pain and your joy
And the pain of a billion people
Begging for safety
And instead getting fear and sorrow
And death

I am so tired

So tired of this position

You both constantly put me in

Both pulling me onto your side

Me, being torn up by the two people I love the most

Both needing me

And me needing to be there for them

It tears me up to see you fight

You are both so right

And both so wrong

With the truth somewhere in the middle

But I can't show that to you

I can only sit watching helplessly

Wanting to grab you both

And shake you till you see

Instead

My heart fills with tiny paper cuts

As you cut each other

Without even meaning to

And I turn away bleeding and exhausted

From being a spectator

In a situation that I do not have the power to change

Gasping for air

Craving companionship

But only from afar

Too close

And it all comes back

The remembering

The story

The vulnerability

The power you have to break me

I needed you tonight

And I asked

And you said you would come

But when I woke up

I was still alone

With all the lights I left on to help guide you home

Still blazing

Alone

Realizing I truly did not matter

Sometimes they break you

The ones you never even wanted

The ones you never even thought about

Until they pushed their way through

And slowly chipped away at that titanium box

The one shielding you from the world

But they chip away

Letting themselves in

Making you trust them

Making you think they care

Until you care back

And this person

All on their own

Makes you believe in love again

And then they are gone

Slamming the door to that box

Just when you wanted to open it more

And the hurt

And the confusion

They leave behind

Makes you wish they had just left you alone in the first place

And makes you question

Why they broke you open

If they never intended to stay

I watch them all move on
All find beautiful others to share their lives with
And I am left in the shadows
Unable to move on
From the fear another brings
From the lack of trust
From the drained state they left me in
From the hurt
I don't think of you
But I think of that
And the hurt outweighs the wanting
And I close the hatch of my titanium box
Pushing myself inside
Where only the loneliness can hurt me

I couldn't drink away the pain

As much as I tried

As much as I wanted to

Enough beers couldn't burn your image

From my mind

Couldn't push me into the arms of someone—anyone- else

Couldn't make me stop believing that you would choose me

All it did was make me miss you more

Make me want you more

And make me hope that amidst the beers somewhere out there you were missing me too

We are all running . . .

Running away from something

The pain probably

The pain that comes with living

That threatens to consume us

Overwhelm us

So we run in the only way we know how

We cope in the only way we know how

Drugs, alcohol, food, exercise, relationships

Whatever distracts us

Whatever makes the pain more bearable

And sometimes our attempts to survive . . . to cope

They kill us

As we learn to deal with the pain

Our method of coping can tear us apart

Until it is too late

And we disappear forever

Whether we wanted to or not

Sometimes we do our best

We give it everything we have

We give with all our strength

And it isn't enough

Life still wins

It overpowers all of our senses

Takes everything that we have inside

Leaving us dark and empty

Scared to be in this place and trying desperately to cope

And sometimes

Our ways of coping in that place

Those are the things that really destroy us

When it is just us, doing the best we can to survive

I watch her cry and question everything

And disappear into a pool of self-loathing

My once beautiful, courageous, kind, loving baby sister

I watch her question every aspect of her being

And live in doubt of her own mystical power

And I want to hold her tight

And whisper softly

I have got you

And he doesn't know anything

And your worth

It does not decrease because he changed his mind

Me alone

It makes sense

I can cope

Hold it together

When it is just me

But me in relation to you

Gets lost

Gets blurred lines

Gets scary

I am flailing

Drowning

When I think of me in relation to you

Because on my own

I am barely staying afloat

Silence

It burns deeper than any words

Waiting to hear from you

Hoping to hear from you

Wanting to hear from you

It hurts less now
A year . . . maybe two have gone by
And the deep ache
It's less sharp, more dull
The anger, it feels less, more subdued
And I think I can go on
But when I see you on the street
I am gutted
And for that moment
I hate you for hurting me
And even more
I hate me for not being enough
And that feeling lingers
Until you are gone again
Brushing past me on the street and walking away
Like you did before
As if I am only a ghost

It's not you
I can't do this anymore
It isn't the right time
This isn't working

Words
I long to hear these words
Any words
To make me understand
What happened?
Where did you go?
Instead . . . Only silence
The gigantic, confusing, exhausting silence
That makes me feel I have disappeared
The kind of silence that's too big to bear
That hurts more than any noise could
The kind of silence
That means I don't matter enough for words

I say I am sorry
*   Again*
Constantly apologizing
For my voice, my appearance, my work
Pushing myself further down
For fear of outshining you
For fear of being seen
For fear of being judged
For fear of saying the wrong thing
For fear of being the wrong thing
Apologizing for any way that my very presence
Could cause chaos or negativity or hurt

I am scared that I could make waves
That I wouldn't be able to handle
That I could get attention with my own light
That I wouldn't be able to handle
That my very presence of being alive would push you away
Which I wouldn't be able to handle
So I shrink
Sink into the shadows
Apologize
So that if I do shine
You know it was an accident

How can you make me feel like
I could light up the world
And then like I am worthless
With only shades of words and silence

Is it possible for me to hurt you more?
I can pretend it isn't intentional
That I am just doing the best I can
To get through each day
But that is a lie
The lie is that I am not trying hard enough
A part of me doesn't want to break the pattern
Of shaking you, of hurting you, of ignoring you, of being angry with you
Day in and day out
Because somehow
That is easier than just being with you and feeling you
My beautiful, terrifying, sensitive, all feeling body

Benign things

They feel like the enemy

Why do I let them have so much power over me?

One thousand steps day in and day out

One thousand cars pass by in the streets

One thousand people walking, talking, living

And all it takes is one

One moment

One decision

From one of those thousands and thousands

Of walkers

Of talkers

Of drivers

To change everything

To shatter our fragile existence

To change the course of the future

One decision

To effect everyone

I don't know how to do this
I don't know how to be here
You slide my shirt off
And my instinct is to run
To hide from your physical touch
To stop you from knowing me
Even though deep down that is all I want

What if I do it wrong?
What if this makes you forget me?
What if this makes you laugh at me?
What if I let you in to the deepest part of me
And you realize
It isn't enough
And you find that I am wrong, flawed beyond measure

That is how I feel
Flawed
Wrong
That you are only part of the waiting game
Here
Until you see me, really see me
And the words fail
And I become your next ghost

I am here
Can't you see me?
Over here
Disappearing in the crowd
Waiting for you
Hoping to be someone worth finding

I want it to be you

You—who I can say all the things to

Good or bad

That cross my mind

And I always apologize

For my vulnerability, my musings, our talks

But really

I know I don't need to

I know you don't mind

And you don't judge

And in some way

Some way . . .

You love me

And I write to you

And I talk to you

And I want it to be you

But more than me

You love her

And I know deep down

That it can never be you

Tonight my breasts hurt
My body is so sensitized
As a part of it awakes
A part that has been asleep for so long
I am ashamed
And uncomfortable
And so unsure of my body
As it tells me that it wants to be alive
When my mind says it isn't sure
And I don't know
What to believe

The tiny ways you pull away

I see them every once in a while

You no longer ask me "how's it going?"

You no longer listen to the music I send you

You no longer invite me to catch up

Those hurt the most

I won't even be thinking about you

When I notice that you have deleted the playlist I made you

And I see you slowly trying to remove me from your life

Without even telling me that is what you are doing

I can't help but wonder what I did wrong

Why you have changed so much

You used to tell me you felt we had known each other forever

Even though it had only been a few months

But now it seems like you are running from forever

Making it as though I don't exist

Trying to erase me from your life in the small ways

Almost so I won't notice

And I will forget you were even there just the way you want to

But I see it

I don't say anything but I see it happening

Feel the tiny movements you make to pull away

And the gut wrenching hurt that comes with each of them

As you decide I am not worth being in this life for you

I am walking because I don't know what else to do

Because if I sit here

And feel the way my body is betraying me

Today especially

Betraying me, changing me

As I beg it to stop

Beg it to let me live on the cusp between not being dead yet and not being fully alive

Beg it to let my body shrink

If I sit here anymore and feel my body decide to be alive

I feel I will die of overwhelm

Because while my body has decided

My brain, my emotions and my soul ... they have not

Do I seem like anyone else?

Put together, calm, happy, ok?

Because the truth is

Everyday is like climbing a mountain or drowning in a whirlpool

And trying, just barely, to stay afloat

Anything to keep breathing

Anything to keep from falling

My truth is that staying alive

Making it through each and everyday is the best I can do

What really separates us from one another?

Why does one get sick and another lives?

Why does one get married, another get divorced and another stays alone forever?

Why does life chew us up and spit us out -

Leaving us gasping for air and safety

When others glide along unscathed?

Why can you be open when I can only zip myself up as tight as possible?

Why does she have to go and we get to stay?

Why must these things insist upon breaking my heart fragment by fragment as I witness

   The love

     The heartbreak

       The suffering

         The longing

           The sadness

             The separation

               The loneliness

The death

As a silent bystander of the life I can't control

It feels impossible
To break through the barricade
The iron shield around my heart
The walls that built themselves without me realizing
Numbing the pain that engulfed me
Over and over and over
Making it more bearable
Making it easier to survive with you, without you
Yet making it impossible to let you in, to let them in, to love you
Even when you are standing right there

Part 3

Day by Day

I write for you

For them

For me

All the things I can't say out loud

The things I am scared to say

That I am not allowed to say

The things I feel in such extremes

Extremes that may not seem appropriate

Extremes that don't seem based in reality

But they are so real for me

Too real

Can't you see it?

It's there, behind my smile

So clear if you looked into my eyes

Even just a small glance, would show you everything

The fear

The confusion

The overwhelm

The things I write

The things we all feel

Do you like me?

Your kindness, your words

They make it seem like you do

Make it seem that you care

About me

For some strange reason

Yet behind those words

You have another life

Another girl

Do you say these things to her?

Do your words make her feel the way I feel?

Or is it just for me?

How do I know?

How do I know if you like me

Or if this is just you

Supporting me the way you support the world

Playing with me

The way you play with the world

It doesn't feel okay
It doesn't feel safe
It doesn't feel like me
But these are feelings
It's okay here
It's safe here
And one day you will feel like you again

You say you are broken

But those who are truly broken

They can't tell

They are so removed from themselves and reality

Everything seems okay

No my love

You are not broken

But you have been cracked

And those cracks hurt like hell

But cracks can heal

Today I work in moments

Get through

One hour

One minute

One second

Don't let it break you

They are only moments

And they will pass

And the need to scream for help will lessen

And the fear of what is happening inside will subside

And tomorrow will be better

Some days
My bones feel brittle
My heart feels broken
My body feels bruised
And I think I will collapse
From this world taking all that I have

Instead I sit here
Alone
Depleted
With nothing left
Still here and still breathing

Do not forget that we are all people
We are all struggling
I hear you
I see you
Keep going

Don't let them dim you
They don't want you
But that is because they can't see
The beautiful human you are
They don't see
The way you are driven by
Love and loyalty and pure human connection
The way you would give up the world
For your co-workers, employees, friends, family
They way you keep us safe, keep us all so safe
They don't see because their minds are driven by other things
Money, wealth, success
Where human beings and relationships
They come second
And they can't see how lucky they are
To have you
But I can see
And when they don't want you
I still do, I will always

Hear me

When you can't hear anything else

Those voices in your head

They are wrong

You are not wrong

You are beautiful and kind

And so very right

It will end
I promise

You may not know this

But I have been there before

I have been where you are

When it was easier to push the knife deeper

Into your own heart

Then to see the love

In your own sister, mother, father, brother

When it seemed like pain was all there was

And all there would ever be

When you convince yourself that this is it

That this heartache will kill you

I have been there

And I am coming back

Because all pain can heal

And all hearts can mend

We are not the broken humans we make ourselves believe

You say I hate you, that I judge you
And I am overwhelmed with despair
Because I desperately want you to know
That I don't
That I love you beyond words
In a way that is so deep in my soul
That I can't even explain it to you
There isn't an action that can show you enough
How deep and visceral my love is
So I try with the words—
They are all I have
They just aren't enough

I know you hurt

I know the pain; the wound is overwhelming

It is all consuming

And all you can see is the pain and the hurt

But I promise to hold the love

Don't push me away

Because you want the pain

Hold me close

So that the love—the love can start to push out the hurt

And one day

It will be a new day

The pain cannot end when we are not on the same team

Do you think we are meant to be?

Even though you have her

And all I have is rejection

Do you think we are meant to be?

Because we can talk for hours

Because I trust you more than anyone I have ever met

Because even though I can't have you

I get butterflies when you walk in the room

Do you think we are meant to be?

Or are we just ships passing in the night

Soul mates from another life

Who are not meant to kiss in this one?

A teacher

A lesson

A test

She told me

Each person who enters your life is one of those

Don't let them break you

Let them show you

He is one of those

Which one?

I didn't want you to choose me
But I wanted to be worth it

Only being here
In this moment
In this pain
In this discomfort
Will help to heal
The wounds I run away from

Yes I feel too much

I love and get left

Yet I can't stop

Because I value human life with my whole heart

I value each and every person on the planet

And when I hear them succeed my whole heart explodes

And when I hear them suffer my whole heart breaks

Like I am being stabbed with a thousand glass knives

Because I can't not give them my everything

I have tried

Life is too fragile for me to lessen my depth of feeling

So when you leave

When you ignore

When you disappear into the shadows taking my love with you

I can't help but feel broken

You didn't know but I gave you my whole heart

As your friend

As your love

As your family

As your stranger

And when you left you took so much of me with you

Maybe without even realizing

In fact, they all did

No words

Can mirror

The way your music

Each melody

Penetrates into my soul

Slicing through the walls I put up

To protect my emotions

To protect my own pain

And in each melody

I feel a cascade of my perfectly boxed up emotions

Slide over me

Well up inside of me

And pour out in tears

As your songs let me feel it

And remind me I am not alone

Talking seems hard today
The weight is so much
It takes all I have just to breathe
To not breakdown
Even though I don't want it to be that way
Please be patient with me

Not even thousands of hours of therapy
Can silence the voices in my head
They are always there
Underlying each thing that I do
Reminding me of what they think I really am
Reminding me that everything is wrong

    My mind

    My body

    My actions

    My relations

They get quieter and louder
But they never truly disappear
They make each day a fight
So that just getting through the day without them derailing me
Is the only thing that matters

The same way you blew into my life
You blew away
As if you had never been there at all
But I was never the same

We have found a way to live
Where survival isn't learning how to find our own food
But learning how to live with our own thoughts
Where we try and fill our days with idleness
To avoid sitting with ourselves
Anyway to avoid the confusion
Of our own minds

My truth is . . .

I feel unsafe; I want to feel safe

I want to feel like a real human again

I want love and support and friendship and people I can really talk to

But instead I feel alone and scared

I don't want to feel lost anymore

I work so hard every day to try and beat this thing

I have come so far, but sometimes I feel like I haven't moved at all

When I think of you

It is as if I have just run ten miles

It is as if a beautiful myriad of colours has exploded in every direction

But a dark cloud swirls in with these colours

Making me doubt all that exists around me

Making me doubt everything about you

And everything about how you feel about me

This mix of colours and blackness swirling inside of me makes my head spin

And my body wants to crumple

And my head wants to explode

As I feel more than I could possibly imagine

All from a few simple words and some loving kindness

It might not be you

But it's the way you make me feel

So special

So wanted

So cared for

So worthwhile

Feelings I lose when I am alone

It's the way you light me up

Just by walking into a room

It's the way you shatter all the walls hiding me from the world

With just one smile

It's the way you bring me back into the world

When I am trying to run from it

It's the way it feels so normal, so comfortable

Just to be around you

It's the way you look at me

And suddenly nothing else matters

All the suffering

> *All the hurt*

>> *All the pain*

For a moment, just a moment you outshine it all

Sitting with it is hard
Sitting with me is hard
Feeling the discomfort of being in my own body . . .
This body . . .
On this planet . . .
It is hard and confusing and oh so debilitating
How can I try and find my space
And my comfort in this body, this home, this world
When it hurts so much

It is like a parade

A parade of them all

All of them who made me believe I was worth loving

But changed their minds

When I wasn't ready to stop loving them

And tonight

They all pass by

Glance in my direction

And pull her in tighter

I thought the cracks they left had healed

But each one that passes in the parade

Breaks open the sewn cracks

Reminding what it is like

To be forgotten

What can I say?
I am not witty
I am not funny
I am not calm
I am not confident
I am terrified
Terrified that you might not like me
That you might run from my words
And even more
That you might actually like me
And my words might make you stay

I am sorry that I can't be more
My body stops me from letting you in
It aches and pains until I take space from you
And I am angry
So angry with it
For stopping me from loving you
From letting you come close
I want to leave my body
Leave all of these sensations behind
And then come and find you
But in the process of hating my body for how I feel
I don't see the protection these sensations hold
Because when I forget, when I am blinded by all of you
My body remembers
That you have hurt me
That I have been hurt before
And that pain is so much worse than any ache or pain my body has
I am sorry that this has made me
And my body
Scared to be open and be vulnerable with you
But I am not sorry
That my body protects me
Even when I don't want it to
I am not sorry my body knows more than I can ever understand
I am not sorry my body makes me and you wait
Tread lightly
Slowing us down
Reminding me that it needs to feel safe
Reminding me no matter how long it takes me to be more, to be open, to feel safe
That should be enough for you

You make my sensitivity feel like a plague

Like it is a disgusting part of me

Because sometimes condescending jokes

They hurt

They cut through my protective layers

Like knife pellets in my heart

Because I know what it is to feel like nothing

I make myself feel like that

And these words –these jokes—they make my own inner insecurities feel a million times bigger

And a million times more real

But amidst that

Really my sensitivity is something beautiful

It allows me to know how I affect others

It lets me connect with the layers beyond our lives

It is such a gift

And when you act like it is not

I hold onto this truth

The truth that I know pain in myself

And because of that I can see the pain in others

And not be part of the world that hurts them more

My heart skips a beat

As I read his words

Another day, another message

So friendly, so genuine

He likes me

And it feels good

And so scary

I read his words

I wonder

Does she see these?

Does she know?

Should I stop?

I didn't want to walk away

But I had to

Because you weren't mine to keep

You were hers

And as perfect as we were

As we would be

As perfect as you were for me

She loved you

And seeing you, talking to you, thinking of you

Left me heavy with guilt

The guilt of ruining your perfect love

So I left

Letting your absence

Not my guilt

Eat away at my lonely heart

You were the one
But with someone else

There came a time when I stopped looking for you

Because all of you—all of them

Were never what I needed them to be

And instead I found you in others

My dad, my sister, my brother, my mother, my friends, my teachers, nature

And you became them

And the you I was told I needed was with me all along

In the supportive trunk of a tree and the gentle whispers of the wind

The longing

For someone that doesn't exist

For someone that I am terrified of

Even if they did exist

For somebody just like you

The you I can never have

The you that brings the longing

And the fear and the lonely

I don't want to hurt
I don't want to feel bad
I don't want to feel forgotten
I wanted you to choose her
I wanted you to stay with her
I never wanted to come between you
I just didn't realize
How my mind and body
Longed for the companionship you gave me

It is amazing that after all this time

And all this work

All it takes is one moment

One trigger

One feeling

For those same fears and emotions and shame and complete overwhelm

To come crashing down on my being

As if they never left at all

Part 4

The Long Road Home

Thank you for reminding me that I am worthwhile
For being excited by my presence
For wanting me to be there
For asking me to be there
When I don't feel worthy

Thank you for thinking I am great
In the genuine soul radiating kind of way that you do
It reminds me that I am here and I am okay
And I am worth something to someone

I dream of you
What it will be like
The kindness, the beauty, the love
You will bring
And the peace, the safety
I will feel
Knowing those years of fighting to keep myself up
Might not be as hard
With you around

It hasn't happened yet
I am not looking for it
Maybe it never will
But at least when it does
I know how it will feel
From my dreams
So very, very safe

There is something more

It calls to me

I can't explain what it is or what it might be

I don't have any idea

But it is there

And it has called

*It keeps me from settling, from being still, **from you***

It promises me more

More than the fear

More than the anger

More than the sadness

More than you

More than we can imagine trapped day in and day out

I must follow it

For being in this with you

Being in this world

Will kill me if I don't

They say we are broken

That our sadness, our anger, our fear, our loneliness, our purest joy

Are because our brains are wired wrong

But what if

Our emotions

Don't mean we are broken

But mean we are more alive than people believe is possible

Maybe it means that we are trying to survive

In the flawed world that we have found ourselves in

Maybe it means that we are so whole

That we can feel when things in life are hard

And wrong

And beautiful

And heartbreaking

Maybe it means we choose not to be numb and oblivious

Not to sail through the days pretending we are okay at all moments

Maybe it just means we are human

I write this for each and every person who has suffered or will suffer at the hands of others or at the hands of their own minds. I see the pain and suffering. I am so sorry that this has happened to you. I am sorry for everyone who this will continue to happen to. I am sorry we have created a place where this is okay.

I hope the words of this book can brings us together—unite us in the emotions that come with being human—the ones that are painful—the ones that we don't want to feel—the ones that make us want to lash out. I hope that the words remind us that we are all struggling—whether it seems like it or not. Let us be united in our pain and our suffering instead of divided. Let us find love to guide us through these challenges, let us find support, let us stray away from violence and pain. Honestly, life is hard enough without the added pain that we impose on each other and ourselves.

Remember that. Remember love. Remember we are all in this together.

You are not alone
xx Alexandra

CPSIA information can be obtained
at www.ICGtesting.com
Printed in the USA
BVHW040219170919
558547BV00012BA/320/P